D0591412

A B C
of Ballet

Edited by
Janet Grosser

Illustrated by
Aline Ordman

DOVER PUBLICATIONS, INC.
Mineola, New York

Bibliographical Note

This Dover edition, first published in 1999, is a slightly altered reprint of *Passport to Ballet: An Illustrated Audience Primer,* originally published by The San Francisco Ballet, San Francisco, California, in 1990. The Introduction and Acknowledgments have been revised and the information about the author and illustrator has been updated for this edition.

International Standard Book Number: 0-486-40871-X

Manufactured in the United States of America
Dover Publications, Inc., 31 East 2nd Street, Mineola, N.Y. 11501

"O body swayed to music, O brightening glance,
How can we know the dancer from the dance?"

William Butler Yeats,
from *Among School Children*,
1926

This book is dedicated to my husband,
Dr. Morton Grosser

Arabesque Penchée
(see page 10)

ABC OF BALLET

INTRODUCTION

ABC of Ballet is an introduction to the language and positions of classical ballet. Enjoyment of dance doesn't require expert knowledge, but, as with other forms of entertainment, knowing more can increase one's pleasure. *ABC of Ballet* is an illustrated primer that explains enough fundamentals to raise your appreciation and enjoyment of this wonderful medium.

The book is arranged in alphabetical order. The most commonly used ballet terms are defined, and many are shown in drawings as well. Defined terms used in other descriptions are indicated by bold italics.

Classical ballet terms are French in origin. As a result a ballet dancer can take class almost anywhere in the world and understand the exercises and combination of steps that the teacher wants performed.

ABC of Ballet was designed to fit in a jacket pocket or a handbag so that it can be taken along to a performance. We hope that this booklet will familiarize you with the basic vocabulary of ballet and add to your viewing pleasure.

THE FIVE FOOT POSITIONS

In the five foot positions the weight of the body is evenly distributed between both feet. The legs are rotated outward (*turnout*), and the knees are straight. All ballet movements begin, pass through, or end in one of these five positions.

First position: The feet are turned out in a straight line with the toes pointing away from each other and the heels touching.

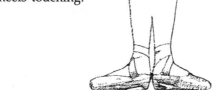

Second position: The feet are turned out in a straight line with the toes pointing away from each other and the heels 10" to 12" apart.

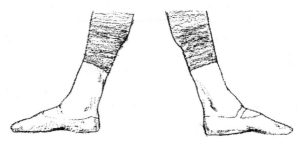

Third position: The feet are turned out, parallel, and partly overlapped. One foot is in front of the other, with the heel of each foot touching the middle of the other.

Fourth position: The feet are turned out and parallel. One foot is about 8" forward of the other.

Fifth position: The feet are turned out and parallel. The right foot is directly in front of the left and both feet are touching, with the heel of one foot next to the toe of the other.

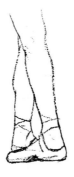

Fifth Position en Pointe:

THE FIVE ARM POSITIONS

While the foot positions are the same all over the world, there are many variations for arm positions. Note that any arm position can be used with any foot position.

First position: The arms are held low and curved, forming smooth arcs out from the sides of the body. The palms of the hands face inward toward the body.

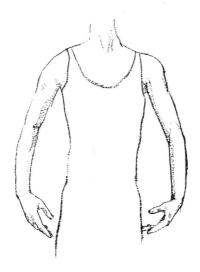

Second position: The arms extend outward sideways from the shoulder. They are held slightly curved down and forward with the palms of the hands rotated partially upward to face the audience.

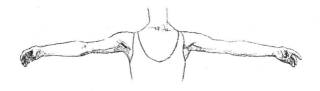

Third position: Either arm is extended in second position. The other arm forms a half-circle in front of the body with the inward-facing hand centered on the breastbone.

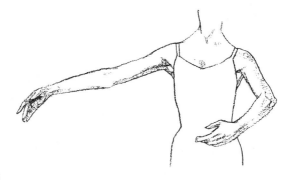

Fourth position: Either arm is curved in front of the body as in third position. The other arm is raised, forming a half circle around the head.

Fifth position: The curved, enclosing arms form an almost complete circle, with the tips of the fingers slightly apart. Like the other arm positions, the fifth can be presented in three variations:

    (1) **En Bas** (ahn bah') with the arms low and the hands close to the thighs.

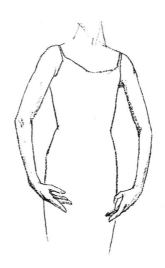

(2) **En Avant** (ahn ah-vahn') with the hands centered in front of the breastbone.

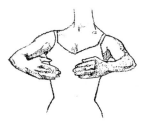

(3) **En Haut** (ahn oh') with the hands raised above the head.

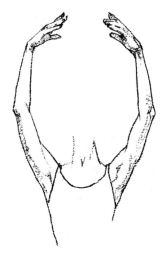

BALLET TERMS

Adagio (ah-dahz′ee-o) A slow dance movement.

Allegro (ah-lay′grow) A dance movement in fast tempo.

Arabesque (ah-rah-besk′) The arabesque is one of the most frequently used poses in ballet. In arabesque, the dancer stands balanced on one leg, with the other leg raised and extended straight behind the body parallel to the floor. The torso is arched forward and upward, and the arms are extended gracefully with the palms of the hands facing down. Arabesques can be done on the flat of the foot, on *demi-pointe* and on *pointe*.

In a first arabesque, the dancer stands in profile to the audience with the arm opposite the raised leg extended forward. The other arm is extended out to the side. In a second arabesque, the body stays the same, but the arms are reversed relative to the legs. In a third arabesque, both arms are extended forward. A downward-tilted arabesque is called an arabesque penchée.

This drawing shows a dancer in first arabesque on pointe, supported by her partner.

Attitude (ah-tee-toode') Attitude is probably the second most often used pose in classical ballet. In attitude, a dancer stands on one leg with the other leg (often called the "working leg") elevated parallel to the ground and bent at the knee. The working leg can be held behind or forward. Usually the arm on the side of the working leg is raised above the head.

At one point in Marius Petipa's *choreography* for *The Sleeping Beauty*, the Princess Aurora moves from a supported attitude on *pointe* (extended leg bent) to an *arabesque* (leg fully extended) with both hands above her head. This is a difficult and beautiful transition.

"My classical ballet background from the age of four has increased my flexibility, overall body awareness, and balance. All of these help me to be a faster and more efficient runner."

Ceci Hopp St. Geme, 1990
1982 NCAA 3000M Champion

Attitude

Attitude Penchée

Ballerina (bah-luh-ree'nah) In the United States, this is a generic term for a female ballet dancer. However, it really should only be used to describe a principal female dancer in a ballet company. In Europe, the leading female dancer is called a *prima ballerina*. In Russia, the most important female star is called a *prima ballerina assoluta*. Many American companies use the term *principal dancer* for their top male and female dancers. *Soloists* are one level down; supporting them are the *corps de ballet*. It takes many years of training and hard work to become a member of the corps, which usually dances in groups. Soloists and principal dancers often begin their careers as members of the corps.

Balletomane (bah-let'o-main) A lover and afficionado of ballet known for his or her enthusiasm and deep interest in ballet as an art form.

Ballon (bah-lawn') The springy, bouncing quality which makes a dancer seem to float in the air during a jump.

"A pas de deux is a dialogue of love."

Rudolph Nureyev, 1965

Barre (bar) The barre is a railing which is fastened to the dance studio wall at about waist height. Dancers hold onto the barre during the beginning of class to do warm-up exercises before going out to the studio floor for center work. Mirrors are placed opposite the barre so dancers can watch themselves during practice. The *barre* is also the sequence of exercises that begins every ballet class.

Battement (baht-mahn') means beating. In ballet, it means the extension of a leg and return to its original position. There are two kinds of battement—*petits battements* (as in *Swan Lake* where Odette performs a series of tiny beats against her ankle), and *grands battements* where the dancer throws a leg as high as possible and down again. *Battements tendus*, where the dancer extends one foot to the side, forward, or back, and then returns it to the original position, are a subset of *petits battements*.

The picture opposite shows a dancer in grand battement. Note—the hands are in *the fifth position en haut* and the dancer is *en pointe*.   ⟶

Grand Battement

Bourrées (boor-ayes') A series of many tiny steps on *pointe* that make the dancer seem to glide across the stage.

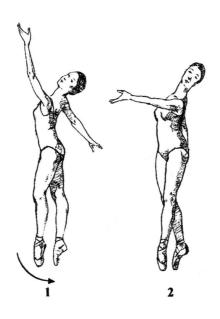

1

2

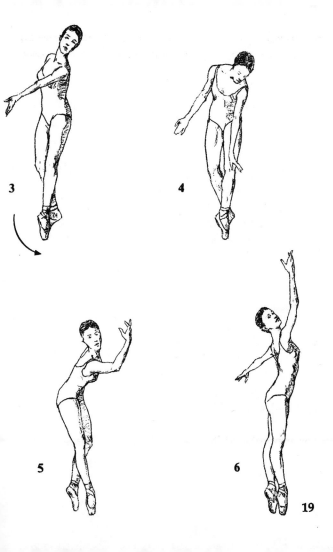

4

5

6

19

Brisé Volé (bree-say' voh-lay') In this spectacular jump the dancer leaps up with the legs fully extended, travelling either forward or backward. The legs beat against each other in mid-air, and the body is arched gracefully before the dancer lands in fifth position. Brisés volés are usually paired, as in the Bluebird's solo in *The Sleeping Beauty*.

Choreographer (cor-ee-og'ra-fer) A person who creates dances by combining patterns of movement.

Choreography (cor-ee-og'ra-fee) is both the craft and art of creating dances, and the movements that comprise a dance.

Coda (ko'dah) A final movement; The finale of a classical ballet.

Danseur noble (dahn-suhr' know'bluh) A more formal name for a principal male dancer. The leading male dancer can also be called the *premier danseur*.

Demi-plié (duh'mee plee-ay') See *Plier*

Demi-pointe (duh'mee pwahnt) See *Pointe*

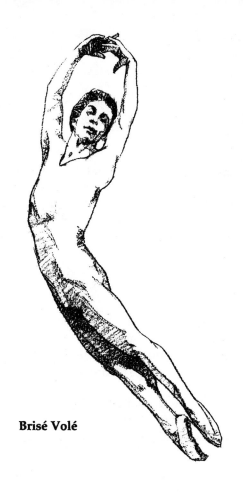

Brisé Volé

Développé (day-veh-loh-pay') The unfolding of the working leg as it rises from the floor and is extended fully into the air.

Élevation (ay-lay-vah'shun) The ability to gain height during springing steps. Also, a dancer's altitude above the floor in a jump.

Fish Dive A spectacular example of partnering in which the female dancer finishes head down in an extended arched curve across her partner. He supports her weight (often almost invisibly) on his thigh, with one arm around her knee.

"Of all the fitness programs I've investigated, ballet seems to be the ultimate challenge."

Roger Craig, 1990
49er Football Star

Fish Dive 23

Fouetté (fway-tay') In a fouetté, a whipping motion of the free leg propels the dancer in a complete turn around the supporting leg. Fouettés are usually done in a series, the most famous example being the Black Swan's thirty-two fouettés in Act III of *Swan Lake*.

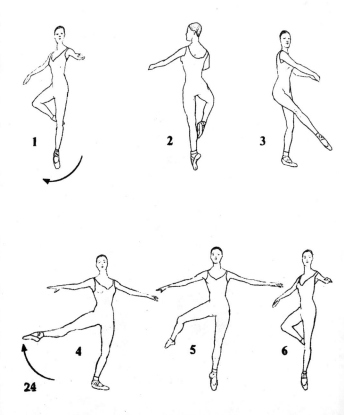

Jeter (zhuy-tay´) means to throw in French. A jeté is a jump from one foot to the other where the weight of the body is transferred from the starting foot to the landing foot. In a *grand jeté* the dancer seems to pause a little in flight, as if defying gravity before landing softly.

Grand Jeté

Mime (meem) The use of gestural expression and movement to tell a story without words. In *The Nutcracker* the Boy Prince uses mime gestures to describe his battle with the Rat King to the Sugar Plum Fairy.

Pas (pah) A dancer's step.

Pas de Chat (pah duh shah') In this jump, the dancer starts from the *fifth position*, goes into a *demi-plié*, and springs like a cat into the air.

Pas de Deux (pas duh duh') A dance or variation for two dancers. A typical pas de deux has four parts: a slow *adagio* for two where the male supports the female; a variation for the *ballerina*; a variation for the *danseur*; and a final virtuosic *coda* for two.

Pas de trois (pah duh trwah') A dance for three people. A pas de quatre is performed by four dancers, and so on.

"Ballet is life. It's always alive, part of a history which we pass on to the next generation."

Violetta Boft, 1990
(Russian ballerina)

Pas de Chat

Pas de Chat

Shoulder Sit

Plier (plee-ay') means to bend. The first exercises at the *barre* each day are pliés. They are used to warm up the legs. Pliés are done in all five *foot positions*. In a **demi-plié** (half plié) the heels are kept on the floor while the body is lowered and the knees are bent slowly and opened wide. Demi-plié in fifth position is used as the take-off and landing position for many jumps. In a **grand** (full) **plié**, the heels are kept on the floor as long as possible while the body is lowered. They may lift off the floor for a moment before the dancer rises to the original position.

Pirouette (peer-oo-wet') A pirouette is a complete turn of the body with the dancer balanced on one foot. The toe of the working leg often touches the knee of the supporting leg. Females usually perform on *pointe* while males use *demi-pointe*. The dancer must remain as vertical as possible. In the past, the term tour was used for the female dancer's pirouette.

In a supported pirouette, the female's partner stands behind her while he supports her lightly at her waist. He can inconspicuously keep her in balance so she can do more turns than in an unsupported pirouette. Often the female will finish a series of supported pirouettes in *attitude*.

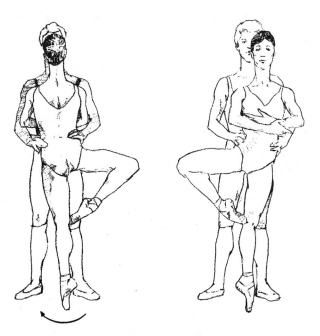

Supported Pirouette

Pointe (pwahnt) Dancing on the extreme tips of the toes. Early ballet was done on the flat foot and on *demi-pointe* (half-point). Dancing on full point was introduced in the early 1800s, primarily as a stunt. Marie Taglioni is credited with transforming ballet on point into an art with *La Sylphide* in 1832.

Port de bras (por duh brah') The carriage and movement of the arms in classical ballet.

Relevé (ruh-leh-vay') To rise from the flat foot on to *demi-pointe* or *pointe*.

Retiré (ruh-tee-ray') In retiré, the toe of the working leg is raised to the level of the other knee and held firmly against the supporting leg at that point. This is the basic position for a *pirouette*.

"I get some kidding when I do a grand tour around the bases, but baseball and ballet are very similar in their need for precise timing and agility."

> **Terry Kennedy, 1990**
> **Catcher,**
> **San Francisco Giants**

Relevé

Sissonne (see-sawn') A jump starting from both feet and landing on one foot.

Spotting This is a technique which keeps a rapidly turning dancer from getting dizzy, and also assists the turn. While the dancer's body appears to spin at a uniform rate, the dancer focuses on one point in the room as long as possible before whipping his head around quickly to the same point. In a perfectly balanced *pirouette*, the whipping of the head can provide enough momentum to keep the body turning.

Toe shoes, or *pointe* shoes, are made by hand, usually to fit a particular dancer, who sews on her own ankle ribbons. The toes of the shoes are reinforced with glue to give support. A professional ballet dancer can use a dozen or more pairs of toe shoes a week.

Tour en l'air (toor ahn lair') literally means a turn in the air. This is usually the province of a male dancer. He'll start in fifth position *demi-plié*, spring directly up in the air, and make as many as three turns before landing in fifth position *demi-plié*.

Turnout The outward rotation of the whole leg from the hip socket to the foot. It takes dancers many years of exercise and practice to attain the full 90° turnout required for classical ballet technique.

"Dance is the hidden soul of the body."

Martha Graham, 1985

Tutu (too'too) The classical ballet skirt, usually made of many layers of net and tulle. The romantic tutu was introduced by Marie Taglioni in *La Sylphide* and ended half-way between the knee and the ankle. The classic tutu reaches to the knee. Over the years, the tutu has been gradually shortened to show the whole leg. The stiff skirt of the contemporary tutu is almost horizontal.

Variation (va-ree-ah-syawn') A solo dance or *Pas seul*.

Swan Position from Swan Lake

PRONUNCIATION OF TERMS

Adagio—ah-dahz'ee-o
Allegro—ah-lay'grow
Arabesque—ah-rah-besk'
Asssoluta—ass-oh-lew'tah
Attitude—ah-tee-toode'
Ballerina—bah-luh-ree'nah
Ballet—bah-lay'
Balletomane—bah-let'o-main
Ballon—bah-lawn'
Barre—bar
Battement—baht-mahn'
Bourée—boor-ay'
Brisé Volé—bree-say' voh-lay'
Choreographer—cor-ee-og'ra-fer
Choreography—cor-ee-og'ra-fee
Coda—ko'dah
Corps—core
Danseur noble—dahn-suhr' know'bluh
Demi-plié—duh'mee plee-ay'
Demi-pointe—duh'mee pwahnt
Développé—day-veh-loh-pay'
Élevation—ay-lay-vah'shun
En Avant—ahn ah-vahn'
En Bas—ahn bah'
En Haut—ahn oh'
Fouetté—fway-tay'

Grand—gran
Grands—grahnd
Jeté—zhuy-tay'
Mime—meem
Pas—pah
Pas de Chat—pah duh shah'
Pas de Deux—pah duh duh'
Pas Seul—pah soul'
Pas de Trois—pah duh trwah'
Penchée—pawn-shay'
Petit—puh-tee'
Plié—plee-ay'
Pirouette—peer-oo-wet'
Pointe—pwahnt
Port de bras—por duh brah'
Premier—pruhm'yay
Prima—pree'mah
Relevé—ruh-leh-vay'
Retiré—ruh-tee-ray'
Sissonne—see-sawn'
Tendu—tahn'do
Tour en l'air—toor ahn lair'
Tutu—too'too
Variation-va-ree-ah-syawn'

SUGGESTED FURTHER READING

Ballet Goer's Guide by Clement Crisp & Mary Clarke. Knopf, 1982

Basic Ballet by Joyce Mackie. Penguin Books, 1980

The Concise Oxford Dictionary of Ballet, Horst Koegler, Editor.   Oxford University Press, Second Edition 1982

One Hundred and One Stories of the Great Ballets by George Balanchine & Francis Mason. Doubleday, 1989

Second Position Arabesque

Janet Grosser received her BS and MS from M.I.T, did graduate work in art at Stanford, and obtained a Masters of Nonprofit Administration from the University of San Francisco. She is a past president of the San Francisco Ballet Auxiliary, and was a member of the board of the International Ballet Council.

Aline Ordman is a Cornell BFA and taught at the Academy of Art College in San Francisco for many years. She currently lives and paints in New Hampshire.